A Thousand Paths to Long Life

A Thousand Paths to
long life

David Baird

MQP

Contents

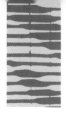

Introduction

We have, each and every one of us, been given a wonderful thing...life! So what are we to make of it and how long will it last? The quality and length of a life depends upon so many factors: the genetics of our species; the genetics of our familial strain; our social environment; our personal lifestyle; our behavior, and in some cases our access or lack of access to certain medical technologies. Some things we feel we can control, and many we feel we can't. Long life, it seems, is a matter of luck and good management. If we follow the advice of current medical thought, eat properly, exercise adequately, take time to relax the mind and body, and, above all, enjoy life, then we are in with a chance.

As we cannot possibly know in advance what our allotted time is, it would be futile to waste whatever lifetime we do have in worrying about it. For centuries, philosophers, poets, scientists, and dreamers have dwelled upon the meaning of life and ways in which we might prolong it. Here in this book, new thoughts united with voices from the past help us in our quest for answers. One thing, however, is absolutely certain—it is up to each and every one of us to make sure that we enjoy our stay here on earth, however long the ride lasts!

What
is Life?

We've all been given one life.
It's ours to do with as we
please—for as long as it lasts.

**Relax and get to know yourself.
Try to understand life and your
part in it. But take it slowly.**

Breathe out the old day and breathe
in the new. We're on our way to a
long life. A life takes as long as it takes.
If you've got nothing to do, what is
life for?

Refocus your perception and see your place in the grand scheme of things.

The miracle is not to fly in the air, or to walk on the water, but to walk on the earth.

When we rise, if our sole intention is to go out and change the world or to improve it, then our life suffers.

Wake up with a desire to enjoy the world—that way you will wake up enjoying your life.

We should be able to leave this life when that time comes without an ounce of talent left. We should use up everything we've been given. We can't take it with us.

Most people are other people. Their thoughts are someone else's opinions, their lives a mimicry, their passions a quotation.

Oscar Wilde

Life is when several billions of cells get together and decide to be you for a while. Enjoy each and every moment, and don't bore the cells!

When we have a why to live
we can bear almost any how.

You will never live if you spend your life looking for the meaning of life.

Some people greet their life as though it were a concrete trampoline.

The moment you discover that the world doesn't have your life but you do, your life becomes a shiny coin which you are free to spend on anything you desire. But you only get to spend it once.

A little bit of
sunshine, freedom,
and a few flowers
is the prescription
for the day.

Don't join the
massed ranks of
quiet depressives
who enter each
day believing life
is a rat race.

Life is a harmless enigma made terrible
by ourselves in our own crazy attempts
to interpret it.

The greatest disease
of these times is
the fear of life.

The secret underlying truth of life is this:
life has no secret underlying truth.

The only wealth is life itself.
That is the greatest wealth—
spend it, enjoy it.

People talk about the cost
of living, but what about the
rising cost of not living?

The simple fact is that life should remain popular, despite the cost of living.

Life has an annoying way of sitting back with its feet up watching us struggle to make sense of things.

All the world's a stage…
all one has to do is figure out the plot.

To a child, the success of a day
is measured by how green the knees
of its pants are.

Some people just hang around,
hoping they'll get used to life.

Determine now to not make your life's end a moment filled with regrets. Or at least make sure they are the right regrets.

Life is a great big canvas, and you should throw all the paint on it you can.

Danny Kaye

How can anyone be truly alive who believes that we are born out of the dark—wet, naked, and hungry, and that from that moment onwards things get worse.

Life is like a beautiful operatic melody, and we add the libretto.

**God pours life into death
and death into life, without
a drop being spilled.**

Why is it that life implies to us great
suffering and effort? Weigh that against
one moment of true love or the
happiness of breathing in a clear new
day, and the other becomes nonsense.

**Each day is a new rough
draft of life's script.**

Life has meaning only if we barter it for something other than itself.

Why torture yourself? Life will do that for you if that's what you want.

There is no wealth but life.

John Ruskin

The price of anything is the amount of life you exchange for it.

You cannot discover the purpose
of life by asking someone else.
The only way you'll ever get the
right answer is by not asking.

The quickest path to an unhappy life is
worrying about why we're unhappy.

**The world owes none of us a
living—it was here first.**

Why do so many of us seek a therapist in our life? Life itself is the most effective therapist available.

Three little words are the sum of a million questions: life goes on.

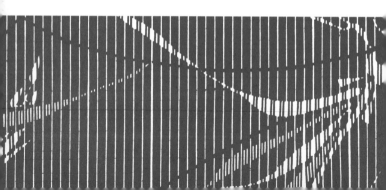

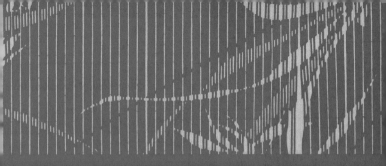

The problem these days is that we're all searching for a book of life that has the answers in the back.

If A equals success, then the formula is: A = X + Y + Z, where X is work, Y is play, and Z is keep your mouth shut.

Albert Einstein

Sometimes questions are more important than answers.

We should give meaning to life, not wait for life to give us its meaning.

If life gives us but one thing, it is an opportunity to gaze at the stars.

In this vast thing called life, all we can ever know is that we know very little about a great many things.

Science is busy staring down through microscopes in a quest for answers, but what if the answer lies on the eyepiece?

There is only one difference between a long life and a good dinner: that in the dinner, the sweets come last.

Robert Louis Stevenson

Everything in life is easier
to get into than out of.

The collision of our life with the future is
what we should look forward to daily.

If we are good we expect life to
treat us fairly, so with that in
mind try explaining to a charging
bull that you are vegetarian.

Some days the best supplement you can take to lengthen your life is a trip to the beauty shop.

When we feel good about ourselves, we feel good about the world and about our life.

Some are afraid of really living their life because they approach it with a fear of getting it wrong.

What is life?
It is the flash of a firefly in the night.
It is the breath of a buffalo in the wintertime.
It is the little shadow which runs across the grass and loses itself in the sunset.

Crowfoot

Life is a comedy that has too
many tragedians cast in it.

**Unbeing dead
isn't being alive.**

                    E. E. Cummings

Anyone can tell you that you must
take life seriously. But can they
provide any evidence whatsoever
that it must be that way?

For goodness' sake don't try and go through life with your focus on the past, in case life runs out in front of you.

The furthest place away
from us is yesterday.

**The most unreachable
place today is tomorrow.**

How much of the past can you hold on to and still have room to embrace the present?

All the riches in the world will not turn back the clock.

If you're stuck on nostalgia, pretend today has already happened, then go out and enjoy it.

Some choose to live life as
a means of avoiding death.

The past is only a guidepost to the future.

Yesterday's happiness turns to
tears if we can't remember it in
the happiness of a new day.

What's so good about the good old days?
The good old days weren't all good.

When one door closes
another door opens; but
we so often look so long
and so regretfully upon
the closed door that we
do not see the ones
which open for us.

Alexander Graham Bell

If you have one eye on yesterday, and one eye on tomorrow, you're going to be cross-eyed today.

Too many fall into their future
while chasing their past.

Some people go through today
carrying the burdens of all their
yesterdays and tomorrows.

Nothing is worth more
than this day. Now.

Rejoice in the things that are
present; all else is beyond thee.

Michel de Montaigne

There can be no eternity if
you choose not to live today.

How many nows are there in forever?

It is only possible to
live happily ever after if
we choose to do it on
a day-to-day basis.

Treat each day as a wonderful new gift. That's why we call today the present!

Without mistakes, life would become tedious.

When each day
is done with us,
we should be
done with it and
quickly let go of
our blunders.
It will not do to
enter a new
day carrying a
burdensome
past.

Tomorrow is a new day; you shall begin it serenely and with too high a spirit to be encumbered with your old nonsense.

Ralph Waldo Emerson

What there is and all there is exists in the present.

The world is filled with people all preparing to live, but never actually living.

Be like a child. Children enjoy the present.

The price of worrying about
what might be and what might
have been is missing what is.

Do you look back in anger?
Go forward in fear?

**Anxiety is our bridge to
the future. Depression is
our bridge to the past.**

The two thieves of life are regret and fear.
If we regret the past and fear the future,
we crucify ourselves between them.

Without a level of self-sufficiency in one's
life, no life can be sufficiently lived.

Those who are mentally
well have the ability to live
in the present moment.

I never think of the future;
it comes soon enough.

Albert Einstein

Those who would live life for
tomorrow will always find their life
one day out of their grasp.

The future
begins now
and now
and now
and...

When the future
gets you down,
make jelly.
That way the
sweet taste
of a yesterday
can be enjoyed
tomorrow in a
moment that
is now.

When we travel through the garden dreaming of the perfect bloom, we tend to forget to smell the roses until it is too late.

Tomorrow has nothing to do with us today. It is sacred ground.

If God had intended us to see where our future paths lead, He would not have made the world round.

Slight not what's near through aiming at what's far.

Euripides

Life itself is not the destination;
it is the journey.

We are born once and there can
be no second birth in this life.

You are not master of tomorrow.

The most fatal form of love
is the love of money.

The most fulfilling form of life
is the love of life.

No joy worthy of the name is obtainable through wealth.

The honest have more peace of mind than anyone. The dishonest always have some reason to feel anxious.

Try not to postpone your happiness, for that is to postpone your life.

The drop of rain maketh a hole in the stone, not by violence, but by oft falling.

Hugh Latimer

Delay is time wasted; such waste of time leaves us no time to enjoy leisure in this life.

One can enjoy glory for a fleeting moment or remain in obscurity forever.

No person can do
better than their best.

No person can become
better than they are without
first becoming who they are.

Listen to others—we can learn
much about our own life from them.

We all have a right to be here.

It doesn't take an Einstein to recognize that in this life not everything that can be counted, counts. And not everything that counts can be counted.

He who has peace of mind disturbs neither himself nor another.

Do not allow your precious life to be ruined by insatiable desires.

The height of pleasure is
attainable here and now.

Let your heart guide you.

Troubles will come
and they will pass.
That is life.

Why
Worry?

What do we do if we want to enjoy a long life? That is one of the perennial questions of mankind.

We go through life asking: What is?

We go through life asking:
Why is there something rather
than nothing?

We go through life asking:
Why is the world the way it is?

We go through life asking:
Where does it all come from?

We go through life asking:
Where does it all go?

We go through life asking:
Where do we come from?

We go through life asking:
Who are we?

We go through life asking:
Where are we going to?

We go through life asking:
What is the purpose of it all?

We go through life asking:
Is there a God?

We go through life asking:
What is good and what is evil?

We go through life asking:
What is knowledge?

We go through life asking:
What is truth?

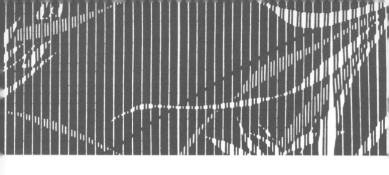

We go through life asking:
What is consciousness?

We go through life asking:
Do we have "free will"?

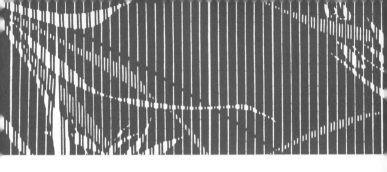

We go through life asking:
How should we act?

We go through life asking:
How can we be happy?

We go through life asking:
What is the meaning of life?

We go through life asking:
What is death?

We go through life asking:
What is after death?

And, of course,
the king of questions:
Why can't we
live forever?

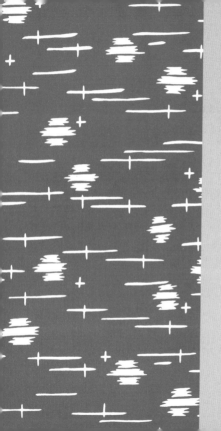

The evolutionary process has programmed us to reproduce, age and die. That is all we're required to do. The rest is up to us.

We physically deteriorate over the course of a life and pray for the miracle of biological immortality.

Why do we find it so impossible to accept the only certainty that there is in life: that we all must eventually die?

The desire for a long life is only the desire to put off the inevitable.

Why should we be afraid of the future? It can only arrive one day at a time.

If we want to live a long life, we must choose to exchange all our imaginary troubles for real ones. Suddenly a sea of troubles becomes a pleasant brook to be crossed easily and at will.

Drag your thoughts away from your troubles…by the ears, by the heels, or any other way you can manage it.

Mark Twain

All that is in the future is not to be feared.

Worry is the nail that punctures the tire of joy.

When you lie awake at night worrying, wouldn't it be better to get up and do something useful? Why not bake bread or a cake?

Remember today is the tomorrow we worried about yesterday.

The misfortunes hardest to bear are those which will never happen.

Rest in the peace of wild things.

Rest in the grace of the world.

Can you recall what it was that you were worrying about on this day a week ago? A month ago? A year ago? A decade ago?

Fear is the main source of superstition, and one of the main sources of cruelty. To conquer fear is the beginning of wisdom.

Bertrand Russell

Worry is not a
safe vehicle.

Don't waste life building bridges
that you will never cross.

The worst mistake is the one
we worry about making.

The demons in our minds are always
far more terrifying than the ones we
meet in life, if we meet any at all.

A person often meets his destiny on
the road he took to avoid it.

Jean de La Fontaine

If you
want to
waste
your life,
worry.

Those who wish to live a stress-free life should cease trying to run the world.

Some people convince themselves that the only time they are actually doing something is when they can worry about it.

Troubles expected and troubles
once had must be dropped if we
are to bear the troubles of now.

While the heart beats,
why worry about it?
When it stops,
why worry about it?

Wake and face each new day—there's no point worrying about yesterday and little point in worrying about tomorrow. So you are free to live today.

Exchange the exhaustion of a day of worry for a week of hard work, and you will get little change.

Worry is
the rust of life.

No worry is
the rest of life.

Worry is a phial of poison seeping into our lives.

Ask any older person how many troubles they have worried about, and then ask them how many of them actually happened.

Nine out of ten troubles
aren't troubles at all.

**My life has been full of
terrible misfortunes, most
of which never happened.**
Michel de Montaigne

Anxiety is a stream in the mind, which if allowed becomes a river of fear, which if allowed bursts its banks and floods all our other thoughts.

Mankind is more often frightened than actually hurt.

Mankind tends to suffer more from imagination than from reality.

It is no good going through life fearing everything that possibly may happen.

The worst worrier worries as he sees life flying past him, and that worries him more.

It is a matter of simple logic: if we fear we will suffer, we are already suffering what we fear.

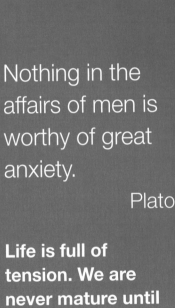

Nothing in the affairs of men is worthy of great anxiety.

Plato

Life is full of tension. We are never mature until we accept this.

The most important time to relax is
when you feel you don't have time for it.

For the sake of getting a living,
we often forget to live.

If we are not careful we will spend
half our life trying to work out methods
of saving time, most of which will
fail anyway.

Work is always twice as important to those who face nervous breakdowns.

Make time
to stand and stare.

The greater
the speed,
the quicker
the death.

We live in a loud and complex world, a world that is constantly trying to knock us out of rhythm with the natural world. We must allow ourselves the chance to return to our rhythm of life.

Leisure is closely linked to the soul.

Why have we allowed ourselves to be convinced that lying on our back on a summer's day in the cool long grass, staring up at the clouds, is a waste of time?

Who says that rest is idleness?

The fellow who never had a day off work in his life died before his time.

Breathe in.
Breathe out.
Rest.
Breathe in.
Breathe out.

Cultivate an awareness that some things are really important, others are not. And make sure you do not get them confused.

If I should die tragically, I would wish that those I love would redress my tragedy in comic garb and try to find some humor in what has occurred.

Imagination was given to man to compensate him for what he is not; a sense of humor to console him for what he is.

Francis Bacon

Live neither in eager anticipation nor fond nostalgia. Live now.

Life is an opportunity—
try to benefit from it.

Life is a beauty—
why not admire it?

Life is a dream—
realize it.

Life is a challenge—
rise to it.

Life is a duty—
to be completed.

Life is a game—
come on, let's play it.

Life is a promise—
to be fulfilled.

Life is
sorrow—
you can
overcome it.

Life is a song—
join in and
sing it.

Life is a struggle—
just accept it.

Life is a tragedy—
to be confronted.

Life is an adventure—
dare to live it.

Life is luck—
you can bet your life on it.

Life is your life—
so fight for it.

A person is only as big as the
dream they dare to live.

Be happy while you're living,
for you're a long time dead.

Scottish proverb

Think. It gives you something to do when your computer has crashed.

Time is nature's way of keeping everything from happening at once.

Too much of anything in life is not good. It is far wiser to have and take things in moderation.

You'll see it when you believe it.

We can all remain young at heart—even if we are slightly older in other places.

Do not regret growing older—it is a privilege denied to a great many.

Education is what you get from reading the fine print. Experience is what you get from not reading the fine print.

If ignorance is bliss, why aren't more people happy?

If it is neither useful nor beautiful, it doesn't belong in your life.

If those who know won't say, then those who don't know will say.

Never let a computer
know you're in a hurry.

Never run after a bus or a person.
There will always be another one.

The things we have are easily
spoiled by our desire for the
things we do not have.

Some people make things happen; some watch while things happen; and some wonder at the end of their life, "What happened?"

What you now have was once
the thing you hoped for.

Throughout life, we should do nothing
that will cause us fear if it were to
become known by anyone else.

Fear and worry eat away at life
until there is nothing but an
empty husk remaining.

The defeated always
learns more than the winner.

Many a life is wasted in prayer for things man can attain by his own power.

Nothing is ever enough for
someone who regards
enough as insufficient.

All arguments, whether short or
long, contribute to the same end.

Learning and pleasure
advance side by side.

Those things that are of the greatest advantage to us are not always the things we can fully understand.

Simplicity and humility are the true attributes of a long and happy life.

Do not keep things locked inside you. Share your joys and sorrows with others.

Temper your desires; let your wants be modest.

You cannot nurture what is with thoughts of what might be.

When things tend to go wrong, we are faced with the choice of going with them or not.

If you nurse
your troubles,
they will grow.

**The greatest pains
in a life spent
worrying are the
evils that never
happened.**

Tension is who you think you should be. Relaxation is who you are.

Chinese proverb

Humor and
Courage

A longer life comes to those who can see the funny side of walking in public with an itch in an unscratchable place.

Humor has a way of bringing people together.

Perhaps we should all begin each day by tickling the person on our left.

Why is it that in a moment of tranquillity something that was so awful at the time can suddenly seem so funny?

When we are able to look on the funny side of life, our irritation and resentment disappear and the day becomes brighter.

A sense of humor is one of the greatest gifts we can possess.

If I had no sense of humor, I would long ago have committed suicide.

Mahatma Gandhi

Perhaps humor is common sense
letting its hair down for a while.

Strip off, look at yourself in a full-length
mirror, and try not to laugh out loud.

Laughter is one of the
most curative gifts given to us.

Those who are able to laugh at
themselves and at the rest of
the world equally outlive us all.

Laughter loves company.

More people are united by something humorous than anything else.

The greatest defense we have against the painted demons and turmoil of life is laughter.

Humor is reason thumbing its nose at the seriousness of life.

Many a serious notion has been
proposed, and accepted,
through comedy.

Humor is when despair
refuses to take itself seriously.

The serious go through life
blowing far too few raspberries.

If you can touch another life for five seconds through humor, the result will last a lifetime.

Humor makes us think, and when we think we live.

There can be no comedy without life.

Life is a comedy; our mistake is that we live it as a tragedy.

Just as tension and worry can be hazardous to our health, humor can be hazardous to our illnesses.

When we cannot find the solution to a problem, the next best thing is to try and find the funny side of it.

It is easier to face the pains and
tragedy that confront us in life
if you wear a smile.

Life without humor is like tap-dancing
on cobblestones with bare feet.

Laughter is the best antidote to stress.

You're never fully dressed
without a smile.

There is nothing so
liberating as laughter.

The greatest gift we can give ourselves in life is a sense of our own ridiculousness.

A smile is the best anti-aging beauty treatment available.

Sometimes laughter is the best defense we have against the cruelty of life.

It takes great courage to say "I'll try again tomorrow" when you've failed at something today.

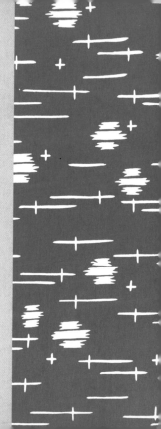

When we have humor we tend to be more courageous in life, and courage provides us with opportunities to use our other virtues.

Courage is not about not having fear; it is about us judging whether something else is more important than our fear.

We betray ourselves when we seek in ourself the courage of someone else. We all have our own courage within us.

The courage we lack the most as human beings is moral courage.

To live is in itself an act of courage.

We do not reach an old age by being fearless. We get there by mastering our fear and by going on despite our fear.

Some of the bravest people who ever lived refused to kill others in wars.

Courage is being afraid but going on anyhow.

**Being too stupid to feel fear
is not the same thing as
being courageous.**

How can we have courage
if we do not also have fear?

**A hero is also someone who is
branded as being a coward for
not doing something when he
knows it may hurt others.**

When our self-preservation mechanism fails us, we are accused of being reckless. When it acts normally, we stand to be called cowards.

Sometimes it is cowardly to go through life being the only one who knows you're afraid.

Courage can't see around corners, but continues its path around them regardless.

It is hard to look brave to an idiot when you run away from danger.

You cannot run away from life.

Our imagination is almost always
our own worst enemy through life,
and it often takes great courage
to ignore it and carry on.

Some have been mistaken
as being brave because they
were afraid to run away.

Courage is the testing point
of all our other virtues.

**The courage of life is often a
less dramatic spectacle than
the courage of a final moment;
but it is no less a magnificent
mixture of triumph and tragedy.**

John F. Kennedy

It takes great courage
to let go of the familiar.

Valor lives in the soul, not in the knees.

Life is, without a doubt, dangerous. We waste a great deal of it trying to prove to ourselves that there is no danger.

Strengthen your resolve
to go on in spite of the danger.

Courage is the firm resolve of virtue and reason.

Steel yourself against the shocks of existence.

The surest sign of maturity
is not to be afraid to live with fear.

Bravery is only varying degrees of fear.

The greatest lesson in life is to
learn how to fear what ought to
be feared and how not to fear
what ought not to be feared.

Courage is knowing what not to fear.

Plato

Courage is being scared to death and saddling up anyway.

John Wayne

Courage takes optimism.

Necessity and courage are twin sisters.

Sometimes our desire to live depends
upon our readiness to die.

A hero is no braver than anybody else;
he is just braver a few minutes longer.

We lead a courageous life when
we do not allow our actions
to be dictated by our fears.

Valor is a gift. Those having it never know for sure if they have it till the test comes. And those having it in one test never know for sure if they will have it when the next test comes.

Carl Sandburg

Courage is a kind of salvation.

Plato

How can we possibly test our courage with caution? It's impossible.

A courageous life is lived by those who, when they know they're licked before they begin, begin anyway.

A courageous life is lived by those who see something through, no matter what.

The most courageous does not always win.

It is all a matter of whether you are frightened before, during or after!

Have the courage to live. Anyone can die.

When you are able to make yourself as you wish to be, you might be better qualified at interfering in other people's lives.

The last judgment takes place every day.

Anyone can carry his burden,
however hard, until nightfall.
Anyone can do his work,
however hard, for one day.
Anyone can live sweetly, patiently,
lovingly, purely, till the sun goes down.
And this is all life really means.

Robert Louis Stevenson

Often those with "good taste" are
less than human and far from alive.

Have courage for the great
sorrows of life.

Have patience for the small sorrows of life.

Accomplish your daily task
and you will accomplish
your life's task.

Go to sleep in peace, and a third
of your life will be lived in peace.

It is better to do well
than to say well.

If you don't know what to say—
say nothing.

Live today by what is true.
That is the best that anyone can do.

Live today by what is true,
even if yesterday's truth turns
out to be a falsehood.

There can be no liberty in life
without discipline.

We can only be free in life when
we are able to contain our desires.

Quite often our lives are shaped by others' opinions of us, brought about by what we say about others more than by what others say about us.

The leisure we enjoy the most
is the leisure we have earned.

If excuses were nails, many of
our houses would fall down.

The first and greatest
victory is to conquer
yourself; to be conquered
by yourself is of all things
most shameful and vile.

Plato

Have the courage to
follow your own path.

Life is a series of battles, internal
and external. To survive, pick
battles big enough to matter and
small enough to win.

Excess on occasion is exhilarating.
It prevents moderation from
acquiring the deadening effect
of a habit.

W. Somerset Maugham

Far too many an apology is ruined by
the inclusion of an excuse.

We should go through life looking at
everything as though we were seeing it
for the very first or the very last time.

Is time that we enjoy wasting, time
wasted?

Have the courage to trust your own
beliefs. Don't be swayed by those
with louder voices.

Often in life the shortcut takes longer than the alternative way. It may look quicker on the map to go over a mountain, but the best way is usually to go around it.

Explaining your life is quite unnecessary, as those close to you have no need of explanation and your enemies will never believe you.

We may feel justified to condemn another's judgment just because it does not match our own, but consider the implications if both are wrong.

Never compromise yourself.

To do nothing is sometimes a good remedy.

Hippocrates

Work out your own salvation. Do not depend on others.

Buddha

I destroy my enemies when I make them my friends.

Abraham Lincoln

The bravest people are often those whose bravery goes undetected.

True courage is silent.

Have the courage to accept the life you have, and the humor to enjoy it.

Relax, laugh, and play. Enjoy life—that is the crucial thing.

Three partners we should never go to bed with are worry, stress, and tension.

Freedom is the greatest fruit of self-sufficiency.

In each of us there is a depth so profound that it remains hidden even from ourselves.

Have the courage to stretch
yourself for greatness.

**Remember to be mortal and that as
such we have a limited span of life.
To enter into discussions about all
things, past, present, and future, is
too big a step for mankind.**

Live life in such a way that you
can leave life with a shout of glory.

Physical courage
often exists in
inverse proportion
to a person's
physical strength.

It takes a brave
man to cry.

Sometimes it takes
greater courage to
listen in silence
than to stand up
and speak out.

Those who go through life believing they have no courage should note that courage does not always manifest itself like some great sword-wielding gladiator.

There is the ordinary life and the extraordinary life. The only difference between the two lives is that one has that little extra to it.

Let your last words be
"I have lived well."

Time the Teacher

To-morrow, and to-morrow, and
to-morrow, Creeps in this petty pace
from day to day.

William Shakespeare

How long a minute is depends
on what you are waiting for.

We are all traveling through life
at the same speed, 60 mph—
that's minutes per hour.

What then is time? If no one asks me, I know what it is. If I wish to explain it to him who asks, I do not know.

Saint Augustine

Time is the wisest counselor of all.

       Pericles

We all crave more time,
yet it is time that we
make the worst use of.

**In terms of a life, the
longest distance between
two places is time.**

Each day is like Christmas—
all those "presents" to enjoy.

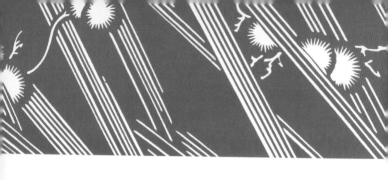

The only way to predict your
future is to create it.

No matter how tall your parents, you
have to do your own growing.

Make your home in your own head
and take it wherever you go.

Life is well spent when you
develop a love of learning.

When you bury the hatchet, don't mark the grave.

Life is made better by having friends you can trust.

There is often more danger in the things we desire than the things we fear.

It is wise to be kind to people on your way up, because you may meet them again on your way down.

Go through life armed with the strength of knowing your weaknesses.

It is no good going through life undervaluing what you are, while others are busy overvaluing what they are not.

Sometimes nothing is better
than the anything they say
is better than nothing.

Once you feel you know everything,
your learning can commence.

We are never so alive
as when we are learning.

The single best thing to teach
a person is how to be curious.

Get onto life's learning curve,
and your life will be a full circle.

Real knowledge is to know
the extent of one's ignorance.

Confucius

There is more to be learned
in a single conversation with
a wise person than years of
study can teach.

Indifference is the blanket
that smothers mankind.

**A repaired error is far
better appreciated
than sterile fact.**

When the student is ready, the
master appears.

Buddhist proverb

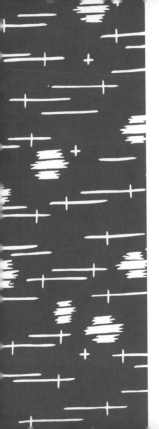

There is as much unlearning to be done in a lifetime as learning.

A life well spent will question all knowledge, not worship it.

The only love affair that we can have that will last a lifetime and not end in tears is one with knowledge.

Exercise your mind regularly with new ideas; it needs to be kept as fit as your body.

Life is spent sailing on a sea of knowledge trying not to capsize in gales of useless information.

Pay attention and you will learn something new every day of your life.

We must try to learn to unlearn what is untrue.

Those who understand everything too soon will never learn anything.

To learn we must
become childlike again.

To learn we must let go of all
our preconceived notions.

For life to lead somewhere
we must allow the lessons
we learn along the way to
nurture our wisdom.

Life ends at whatever age we selectively stop learning.

Anyone can view the sea of knowledge from the shoreline of wonder, but few are brave enough to take the plunge.

We learn little from those who agree with our every word.

We should learn a lesson in life, and in learning, from computers. A computer can learn, unlearn, and relearn without the ego getting in the way.

There is a great deal more to be learned in life by struggling to find an answer than from being given the solution.

True understanding only comes from learning about something from every angle.

Without a goal in sight,
all you will see are obstacles.

Shoot for the moon.

Those who go through
life knowing exactly
where they are going
never get the chance to
end up somewhere else.

Live a fulfilled life upon which you can look back and reflect upon what you have done, not a life where all you can look back upon is what you might have done.

If everybody considered only what is possible, some of the most impossible feats would never have been accomplished.

You have to construct a door before opportunity can knock on it.

A life
goal is a
dream
with a
deadline.

How would it be possible to find out
how far we can go in a lifetime without
occasionally risking going too far?

A life is spent making opportunities
and finding a few along the way.

A deadline is useful to those
who lack inspiration.

You can climb life's ladder to get to the top, but once there you have to keep climbing.

In sleep your dreams may seem true,
but to make them them come true you
have to wake up and get out of bed.

**When you give your idea wings,
don't forget to include landing
gear as well.**

There are great things beyond our capability to do, and some small things which we refuse to do. The important thing is not to not do.

If life will let you, who is going to stop you?

Life is full of optical illusions.
Life is full of obstacles.
Life is full of obstacle illusions.
Life is full.

Does there ever become a point where it becomes too late to become who we might have been?

Ninety-nine percent of life seems to be spent making last-minute changes.

Seventy percent of success in life is showing up.

Woody Allen

Many a life is wasted by those who sit and think about how to live it for longer.

One person's impossible is another person's challenge.

Adventure follows vision.

I am looking for a
lot of men who have
an infinite capacity
to not know what
can't be done.

Henry Ford

We would be better off if we spent as much time learning the trade as we do learning the tricks of the trade.

Few places that are worth reaching have shortcuts leading to them.

If we are honest with ourselves, something is either done or not done by us. Trying to do something means nothing.

Often it is the rules that get in the way of accomplishment.

Mankind rarely fears the distance—it is the first step that is feared.

There is a fine line between insanity and genius—these days, one can be successful at both.

If you have built castles in the air, your work need not be lost; that is where they should be. Now put the foundations under them.

Henry David Thoreau

The storm of doing is always
followed by the calm of done.

Most people would succeed in
small things if they were not
so downright ambitious.

A life wasted is one spent doing
something efficiently that should
never have been done at all.

In the garden of problems, you have to get to the roots.

Many are stubborn in pursuit of the path they have chosen, few in pursuit of the goal.

Friedrich Nietzsche

Even if we're not where we're going, at least we're not where we were.

One person's goal
is another's starting point.

**The young annoy their elders
generation after generation
by attempting the impossible
and achieving it.**

If you would hit the mark, you must aim a little above it; every arrow that flies feels the attraction of earth.

Henry Wadsworth Longfellow

It is possible to miss the mark by aiming too high just as it is to aim too low.

How do I do so many things? Why do you do so little?

Look back through history and consider the extraordinary things one person can achieve in a lifetime—and be inspired.

When we are younger we go off searching for ourselves, allowing others to convince us of who and what we are, instead of asking of ourselves the questions only we can answer.

You cannot live a long life when
you treat it as if it will go on forever.

The most important person
not to fool is yourself.

I am nobody but myself.

There are few who live long who don't end up feeling that the life they have lived was meant for somebody else.

And remember: no matter where you go, there you are.

Confucius

Life is a journey,
and only you hold the map.

We waste our lives when we spend
more time attempting to be a pale
imitation of somebody else than we do
in becoming ourself.

Unless we are careful, we will spend so much time disguising our true self to others that we will never recognize our true self ourselves.

We are not all born to be poets, but we are each of us a poem.

Every person wastes part of their life attempting to display qualities which they do not possess.

Would you
recognize
yourself if you
bumped into
yourself in
the street?

The first major step to a long life is to decide now not to be something but to be someone.

Learn to be what you are, and let go of all those things that you are not.

There is just one life for each of us: our own.

Euripides

Hateful to me as the gates of Hades is that man who hides one thing in his heart and speaks another.

Homer

Life is yours: accept nobody's definition of your life.

Life is yours: don't waste a moment.

Life is yours: define yourself.

Life is yours: never allow yourself to be bullied into submission or silence.

Life is yours: do not allow yourself to be made a victim.

When you display your true feelings, there should be no need for apologies.

If God had wanted me otherwise, he would have created me otherwise.
Johann Wolfgang von Goethe

Wherever you go,
go with all your heart.

Confucius

**Let the world come to
know you as you are.**

What is a clock if not an instrument of torture, ticking away, slaying time, and stealing life.

Killing time is injurious to eternity.

Killing time is impossible.
It is time that kills us.

They say time flies,
but it is we who
fly past time.
Time remains;
it is we who go.

The shortest hours are
the ones between work
and sleep.

If we could make every
moment in our lives count,
that indeed would make
for a long life.

The richest person alive is the one who uses the time most other people throw away.

It takes quite a lot of courage for us to grow up and become who we really are.

Do not try to be all things to all people. Begin by being yourself to yourself.

Time treats us all the same. No matter how much wealth or influence or power we have, the day is the same length for all.

Opportunity hides in the most unlikely places.

Next time you feel there isn't enough time to do something, remember that your day is no shorter than Michelangelo's, Leonardo da Vinci's, Albert Einstein's…

Time, they say, is
a great teacher,
yet it kills all its
students at some
time or another.

Young
and Old

We are all of us born into this world with a need to be loved, and we will never in all our days outgrow it.

Life is spent grasping at kisses and meanings.

No baby is an it.

Babies are our most important link with the future.

A man may be born, but in order to be born he must first die, and in order to die he must first awake.

Georges Gurdjieff

I was born. Do not say it lightly. Consider the depth of that statement. It represents the creation of an everlasting living soul, something that will last for all eternity.

What those before us began is now our own.

When we are born, we cry that we are come to this great stage of fools.

William Shakespeare

When we try to prolong our childhood, life gets more difficult.

Childhood is the opening in the low garden wall that lets us into the magical mystery world of the future.

We outgrow many childhood things, but will never lose the images and stories of childhood.

What makes being a child so different to being a grown-up? It's fun.

Children aren't dumb. They know the difference between a toy with a motor and a vacuum cleaner.

Felicity and children
walk hand in hand.

Children trust life.

There is no finer
investment
for any
community than
putting milk into
babies.

Winston Churchill

We are far too swift in criticizing children when we should be providing them with the models they need for life.

The best way to get something done is to forbid a child to do it.

The worst blow to any grown-up is to be disliked by children.

Children learn far more from observing how adults live than they do from what adults have to say.

Grown men can learn from very little children, for the hearts of little children are pure. Therefore, the Great Spirit may show to them many things which older people miss.

Black Elk

It is dangerous to confuse children with angels.

Alas! regardless of their doom,
The little victims play!
No sense have they of ills to come,
Nor care beyond to-day.

Thomas Gray

When children deserve our love the least,
that is when they need it the most.

We may at some time in our lives enter
what is called a second childhood, but our
youth comes around only once.

Our main problem is that we all too easily forget what it is like to be a child. Children are as unpredictable as adults are inconsistent.

A child miseducated is a child lost.

John F. Kennedy

We should not handicap our children by making their lives too easy. Too often we give children answers when we should be giving them problems to solve.

What is needed is a little less worry over the child and a bit more concern about the world we make for the child to live in.

Children are the makers of men.

Where children are, there is the golden age.

Novalis

How little is the
promise of the child
fulfilled in the man.

Ovid

**You can tell
when children
are growing up
through the kinds
of questions they
ask. Suddenly
they become
answerable.**

There is never a dull moment in watching children grow up. It's a link with our own childhood and everything else becomes insignificant.

The training of children is a profession, where we must know how to waste time in order to save it.

Jean-Jacques Rousseau

Children, in their own minds at least, have an incredible knack of completing to their own satisfaction every task they set themselves.

In great countries, children are always trying to remain children, and the parents want to make them into adults. In vile countries, the children are always wanting to be adults and the parents want to keep them children.

John Ruskin

Children wish fathers looked but with their eyes; fathers that children with their judgment looked; and either may be wrong.

William Shakespeare

To a child, the simplest journey becomes an adventure.

Adults are incredible—they'll do anything for their children except stay married to their mate.

Look at a child and there you will see a world of possibilities and potential.

Children are the eyes of tomorrow.

Youth is surely wasted on the young.

Try to live up to the trust of a child.

While you concern yourself about what your child may or may not be in the future, don't forget that the child is someone right now.

Probably the happiest period in life is in middle age, when the eager passions of youth are cooled, and the infirmities of age not yet begun; as we see that the shadows, which are at morning and evening so large, almost entirely disappear at midday.

Thomas Arnold

The surest sign of age catching up with us is loneliness.

The young are slaves to dreams; the old servants of regrets.
The most difficult art is the art of growing old without regret.

You're only as old as you feel.

You've got to start young at old age if you're ever going to get it right.

If all those who lied about their age had children, there would be three times the number of illegitimate children in the world.

There is no feasible way of living a long life without aging.

Men of age object too much, consult too long, adventure too little, repent too soon, and seldom drive business home to the full period, but content themselves with a mediocrity of success.

Francis Bacon

A sure way to stay clear of old age is to program yourself to the notion that old age is always ten years older than you.

The body may age, but in our minds we are always about sixteen years old. That is our blessing and our tragedy.

We do not grow old, we become ourselves.

I hope I never get so old I get religious.

Ingmar Bergman

Therefore we do not lose heart. Even though our outward man is perishing, yet the inward man is being renewed day by day.

2 Corinthians 4:16

Exercise, study, and love—
that is the way to really live.

To live long and to end life well,
this seems to be both our quest
and our burden.

Grow old along with me!
The best is yet to be.

Robert Browning

We should so provide for old age that it may have no urgent wants of this world to absorb it from meditation on the next. It is awful to see the lean hands of dotage making a coffer of the grave.

Edward G. Bulwer-Lytton

Age means a lot to some, particularly when it comes to wine or cheese.

Those who think they have learned everything by a certain age have difficulty remembering it all from that point onward.

Have you ever stopped to notice just how beautifully leaves grow old? Consider how full of light and color they become in their last days.

We are not what we were—but that is something to be celebrated, not mourned.

It was one of the deadliest and heaviest feelings of my life to feel that I was no longer a boy. From that moment I began to grow old in my own esteem, and in my esteem age is not estimable.

Lord Byron

Be certain that every time you feel that life has ended, something else happens.

In youth we turn off the lights for romantic reasons. In old age we turn it off for economic reasons.

When you consider the alternative, suddenly old age doesn't seem bad at all.

We can feel younger for longer by correcting our diet, using antioxidants for the removal of toxins from our body, by taking regular exercise and practicing yoga and by utilizing breathing techniques and meditation. Or we could just get on with living.

No one is so old as to think he cannot live one more year.

Marcus T. Cicero

Age is a matter of feeling, not of years.

In life there are only two truths: your ability and your failing.

No people are so piteous and forlorn as those who are forced to eat the bitter bread of dependency in their old age.

The thing about age is it isn't about how old you are, but how you are old.

In the name of Hippocrates, doctors have invented the most exquisite form of torture ever known to man: survival.

Luis Buñuel

Do not count a person by their years, but rather by the things they have done in those years.

Those who love deeply never grow old; they may die of old age, but they die young.

Benjamin Franklin

Age does not make us childish, as some say; it finds us true children.

Johann Wolfgang von Goethe

The moment we begin to dislike ourselves, we become the oppressed minority.

The spirit should never grow old.

The value of old age depends upon the person who reaches it. To some men of early performance, it is useless. To others, who are late to develop, it just enables them to finish the job.

Thomas Hardy

When we are young we lie about our age and try to put ourselves across as being a little older. When we reach a certain age we begin to lie again and try to put ourselves across as being a little bit younger. We are never satisfied with our age.

Forty is the old age of youth, fifty is the youth of old age.

Victor Hugo

Go to bed and sleep whenever you feel compelled to sit up and worry.

Work is always stimulating, rejuvenating, exciting, and satisfying.

It would appear as if most people don't know how to be old.

Why shouldn't eighty-year-olds
throw snowballs?

It's only the body that changes—
within, we remain ourselves.

Life, like cheese, improves with age.

From the summit of our old age, we
can either look ahead at the next
mountain we will climb or look
back down from whence we came.

**From the middle of life onward,
only he remains vitally alive who is
ready to die with life.**

Carl Jung

You can sit down and wait for
old age to catch you up, or get
up and get out and start walking
in the opposite direction.

The elder Cato, it is said, began to learn Greek at the age of eighty. That is optimism.

Don't count your years; make your years count.

Don't let the breeze become a gale.

Most bad habits are tools
to help us through life.

Every new idea has a
modicum of pain attached to it.

Drink to life—to all it has
been, and to all it will be.

A person is not mature until he has both an ability and a willingness to see himself as one among others.

The days seem long and the years seem short; quite the opposite to when we were younger, when no day was ever long enough and a year was an eternity.

Teach the world to admire wrinkles as the etchings of experience.

Gray hairs are signs of wisdom.

We pay for the excesses of our youth if we live to grow old.

The older the fiddler, the sweeter the tune.
English proverb

It seems that the older we get
the older we want to get.

With mirth and laughter
let old wrinkles come.

William Shakespeare

If you can't laugh about life, what use is it?

It is strange how everybody wants to
live long but nobody wants to be old.

The oldest living people are those who have outlived enthusiasm—whether they are fifty or one hundred years old.

The most unexpected thing that can happen to a person is old age.

Methuselah lived to be 969 years old,
and yet we have seen more changes in
the past fifty years than he did in his
entire life.

Curiosity and enthusiasm are the
greatest aids to longevity.

In every human being's heart there is
the lure of wonder and the joy of living.

Allow yourself to enjoy the age you are, with neither regrets for the past nor anxieties for the future.

Old age, calm, expanded, broad with the haughty breadth of the universe, old age flowing free with the delicious near-by freedom of death.

Walt Whitman

Instead of worrying about whether or not you will be here tomorrow, enjoy today.

With age comes the contentment of looking back on the accomplishments we once hoped for.

Old age is an exclusive club where not everyone will be lucky enough to qualify for membership.

We become old on the day we forget our past blessings.

We must not resist Nature, but submit to her and learn from her.

To stay young, eat well, sleep well, exercise well, and lie about your age.

Oh, what a day-to-day business life is.
Jules Laforgue

Remember: all old men were once young, but not all young men will safely reach old age.

Resolve

You cannot discover the purpose of life by asking someone else—the only way you'll ever get the right answer is by asking yourself.

He who has nothing to die for has nothing to live for.

Human life is purely a matter of deciding what's important to you.

It is your right to exist on this earth and choose your way of living.

Don't let yesterday use up
too much of today.

If you are still talking about
what you did yesterday, you
haven't done much today.

Peace lives somewhere between
trying to relive the past and
worrying about the future.

The past is a good place to visit,
but I wouldn't want to live there.

One thing is fact: if you worry about tomorrow, tomorrow comes. If you don't worry about tomorrow, tomorrow comes.

Ask yourself what you might do each day that will allow you to feel more alive during your waking hours.

Budget an hour in your day just for yourself, and use it just for that.

Do something, do anything, but don't do nothing at all.

Worry is a complete cycle of inefficient thought revolving about a pivot of fear.

Blessed is the person who is too busy to worry in the daytime and too sleepy to worry at night.

The mark of a successful man is one who can spend an entire day on the bank of a river without feeling guilty about it.

Worry often gives a small thing a big shadow.

Every survival kit should include a sense of humor.

A man of courage never wants weapons.

It is easy to be brave from a safe distance.

Aesop

The braver the arm, the longer the sword.

Those who live are those who fight.

Victor Hugo

Never miss an opportunity to make others happy, even if you have to leave them alone in order to do it.

Don't look where you fall, but where you slipped.

God gave us two ends—one to sit on and one to think with. Success depends on which one you use.

Giving up doesn't always mean you are weak. Sometimes it means that you are strong enough to let go.

Promise only what you can deliver.
Then deliver more than you promise.

When you lose, don't lose the lesson.

Be inquisitive.

To know the road
ahead, ask those
coming back.

Chinese proverb

The past is already past.

The future is not yet here.

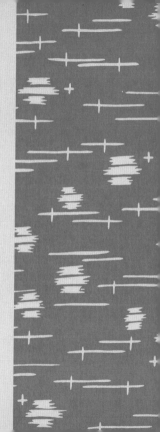

Things are constantly changing.

Appreciate the past, look forward to the future. Live in the now.

Do not retain your timeworn views; embrace the new.

Reflect within yourself—that is where your strength lies.

The self has no boundaries except those it accepts.

The purpose of life is being—
as opposed to not being.

Never give consideration to things
you do not wish to happen.

As long as we allow ourselves to be motivated by greed and gain, there can be no peace.

You must learn to listen to the voice of the inner self.

Though no one can go back and make a brand-new start, we can all start now and change the outcome.

Each of us creates our reality according to our beliefs, our expectations, and our actions.

No dream is too big
that we can't
grow into it.

**Knowledge is
haunted by the
ghost of past
opinion.**

If you don't have time
to do it right,
you must make time
to do it over.

**Know your limits—
but never stop
trying to exceed
them.**

When you throw dirt, you lose ground.

Opportunities are never lost—someone
will always take the ones you miss.

Some of us are far too busy mopping
the floor to turn off the faucet.

If you aim at nothing,
you'll hit it every time.

Vision without action is a daydream. Action without vision is a nightmare.

When the horse is dead, you'll get further if you get off it.

There is a lot more juice in a lemon than meets the eye.

Those who forget the pasta are condemned to reheat it.

There's more to truth
than the facts.

Even the broken clock
is right twice a day.

When the student is ready,
the master appears.

Buddhist proverb

Grandmas are moms with lots of frosting.

We live in an age when the truth is so poorly lit that it becomes almost impossible to become enlightened.

Before enlightenment—
chop wood, carry water.
After enlightenment—
chop wood, carry water.

Zen Buddhist proverb

Knock on the sky
and listen to the sound.

Zen saying

The enlightened see life as
an opportunity to become
more enlightened.

When you buy a doughnut,
don't forget to eat the hole.

You can't wake a person
who is pretending to
be asleep.

Our greatest fortune lies in our inner vault. Within is everything we could ever need.

Concealment can only ever be temporary.

Necessity is an evil, but the greater evil is the necessity for continuing to live subject to necessity.

No one sets out to choose a thing because it is evil, but we are often caught in the trap of accepting the lesser of two evils.

Dwell on your friends, not on the advantages of friendship.

When we travel through life with good friends around us, even if we never need their help we can be confident of their help in need.

There is no good reason for ending a life, especially one's own.

If you chase two rabbits, you won't catch either.

You can't fall off the floor.

Sometimes a stumble may prevent a fall.

A wise man
can see more
from the
bottom of a
well than a
fool can from a
mountaintop.

Philosophy is nothing but common sense in a natty suit.

When we waste time, we kill life.

Let not the sands of time
get in your sandwiches.

Live today, for tomorrow
it will all be history.

Learn from yesterday, live for today,
hope for tomorrow.

Those who live poor die rich.

Making a life comes before making a living.

Do those things living that are desired when dying.

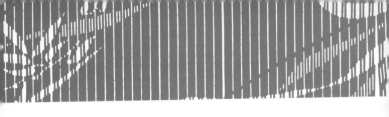

No one ever said on their
deathbed that they wished
they'd spent more time
at the office.

**Always remember that we
live in two worlds—one that
we can see and one that
remains invisible.**

A full pocket is not worth the price of your soul.

Use wisely the things that we have been enabled to fashion out of nature's raw materials.

Self-respect has somehow become diluted by the notion of self-esteem. Given that respect is something earned, how much do you respect yourself?

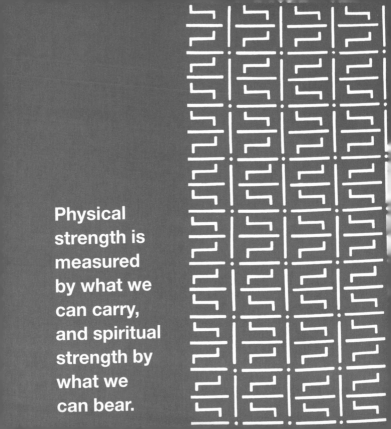

Physical strength is measured by what we can carry, and spiritual strength by what we can bear.

Someone whose life is all show
has no self.

We can choose to be true to ourself
and risk the ridicule of others, or to be
false and risk losing our self-respect.

Who can stand anything in life
if he cannot stand himself?

It is better to displease the people by doing what you know to be right than to temporarily please them by doing what you know to be wrong.

Life does not cease
to be funny when
people die any
more than it ceases
to be serious when
people laugh.
George Bernard Shaw

Only a few things are
really important.

**If death is Shhh...
then life should be
Whooppee!!!**

Dare to join in the
cosmic dance
that is life.

The philosophy of one
century is the common
sense of the next.

Generosity and perfection
are everlasting goals.

Don't be hasty; prosperity will knock on your door soon enough.

The surest route to a life of torment is to believe that all things happen by necessity.

Place your pride in your own qualities and not your external circumstances.

Bad habits are no different to evil people who would do us harm.

The noble man is chiefly concerned with wisdom and friendship. Wisdom is good for a lifetime; friendship is good for eternity.

Let the goals you set for your life be the criteria for all decision-making, and you will rarely become over-whelmed by doubt or confusion.

You have an active mind and a keen imagination. Use them.

Better to light a candle than to curse the darkness.

You can always find peace in silence.

If you are patient in one moment of anger, you will avoid one hundred days of sorrow.

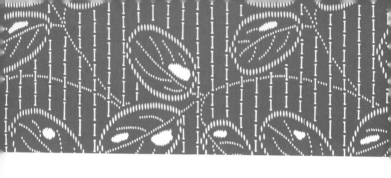

Life is filled with gentle
hints to help you make
decisions. Heed them.

A friendly heart will gain many admirers.

While we come closer to realizing that the universe might not after all be infinite, we have grown positive that man's stupidity probably is.

A greedy heart is a heavy burden; it is never satisfied.

Tact is the most welcome guest
at all occasions.

Be certain that your lies will cross
the finishing line before you.

Your determination will take you
where you want to go.

The worst separation of all is that which occurs between a person's income and their lifestyle.

Chances are
for taking,
not just for
considering.

Believe in your physical powers and they will increase.

Don't seek your life in someone else's.

Listen to your body—it will tell you what it needs to survive. Don't let your mind force your body to do reckless things.

We are all born with the courage within us to surmount any obstacles that might fall in our path.

People who say that it cannot be done should not interrupt people who are doing it.

The art of living is a series
of letting go and holding on.

Living a long life and living
a long, active life are not
the same thing.

When we are born we are given the raw materials with which to create a wonderful work of art of life or a complete pig's dinner. The choice is ours.

Philosophies

Begin at the beginning...and go on till you come to the end; then stop.

Lewis Carroll

I am a part of all that I have met.

Alfred Lord Tennyson

Believe those who are seeking the truth. Doubt those who find it.

André Gide

Beware lest you lose the substance by grasping at the shadow.

Aesop

The obscure we see eventually. The completely obvious, it seems, takes longer.
Edward R. Murrow

Many men go fishing all of their lives without knowing that it is not fish they are after.
Henry David Thoreau

You never know what is enough, until
you know what is more than enough.

William Blake

**Think like a man of action,
act like a man of thought.**

Henri Louis Bergson

The fly that doesn't want to be swatted is
most secure when it lights on the
fly-swatter.

G. C. Lichtenberg

It is better to know some of the questions than all of the answers.

James Thurber

Alice came to a fork in the road.
"Which road do I take?" she asked.
"Where do you want to go?"
responded the Cheshire cat.
"I don't know," Alice answered.
"Then," said the cat, "it doesn't matter."

Lewis Carroll

No man ever steps in the same river twice, for it's not the same river and he's not the same man.

Heraclitus

Almost every wise saying has an opposite one, no less wise, to balance it.

George Santayana

It is best to rise from life as from a banquet, neither thirsty nor drunken.

Aristotle

The opposite of a correct statement is a false statement. But the opposite of a profound truth may well be another profound truth.

Niels Bohr

Proverbs often contradict one another, as any reader soon discovers. The sagacity that advises us to look before we leap promptly warns us that if we hesitate we are lost; that absence makes the heart grow fonder, but out of sight, out of mind.

Leo Rosten

The charm of history and its enigmatic lesson consist in the fact that, from age to age, nothing changes and yet everything is completely different.

Aldous Huxley

Genuine tragedies in the world are not conflicts between right and wrong. They are conflicts between two rights.

Georg Hegel

Beware the fury of a patient man.

John Dryden

If a man will begin with certainties, he shall end in doubts, but if he will content to begin with doubts, he shall end in certainties.

Francis Bacon

The future influences the present just as much as the past.

Friedrich Nietzsche

What is man, when you come to think upon him, but a minutely set, ingenious machine for turning, with infinite artfulness, the red wine of Shiraz into urine?

Isak Dinesen

Most human beings have an almost infinite capacity for taking things for granted.

Aldous Huxley

I can't help it, the idea of the infinite torments me.

Alfred de Musset

You only have power over people as long as you don't take everything away from them. But when you've robbed a man of everything he's no longer in your power; he's free again.

Alexander Solzhenitsyn

To see a World in a Grain of Sand,
And a Heaven in a Wild Flower,
Hold Infinity in the palm of your hand,
And Eternity in an hour.

William Blake

Live as long as you may, the first twenty
years are the longest half of your life.

Robert Southey

Life's short span forbids us to enter on far-reaching hopes.

Horace

Do not try to find out—we're forbidden to know what end the gods may bestow on me or you.

Horace

Five minutes! Zounds! I have been five minutes too late all my life-time!

Mrs. Hannah Cowley

Have not the wisest of men in all ages, not excepting Solomon himself, have they not had their Hobby-Horses and so long as a man rides his Hobby-Horse peaceably and quietly along the King's highway, and neither compels you or me to get up behind him, pray, Sir, what have either you or I to do with it?

Laurence Sterne

On with the dance! let joy be unconfined;
No sleep till morn, when Youth and Pleasure meet
To chase the glowing Hours with flying feet.

Lord Byron

Drop the question what tomorrow may
bring, and count as profit every day
that Fate allows you.

Horace

How beautiful is youth, that is always slipping
away! Whoever wants to be happy, let him
be so: about tomorrow there's no knowing.

Lorenzo de' Medici

If I have seen further it is by standing on the shoulders of giants.

Sir Isaac Newton

My soul, do not seek immortal life, but exhaust the realm of the possible.

Pindar

One should eat to live, and not live to eat.

Molière

**...Life goes not backward
nor tarries with yesterday.
You are the bows from which your
children as living arrows are sent forth.**

Kahlil Gibran

In our lifetime we will all say something
great. Whether we were the first to say it or
not is immaterial. The essential thing is that
we and those who hear it recognize its
greatness and allow it to echo through time.

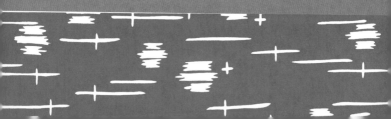

How often are we to die before we go
quite off this stage? In every friend we
lose a part of ourselves, and the best part.

Alexander Pope

Every man, when he comes to be sensible
of his natural rights, and to feel his own
importance, will consider himself as fully
equal to any other person whatever.

Joseph Priestley

**Bring down the curtain,
the farce is played out.**

François Rabelais

It is perfectly certain that the soul is immortal and imperishable, and our souls will actually exist in another world.

Plato

While we're talking, envious time is fleeing: seize the day, put no trust in the future.

Horace

When you look into an abyss, the abyss also looks into you.

Friedrich Nietzsche

We should not seek to follow in the footsteps of the wise. We should be seeking what they sought.

When he that speaks, and he to whom he speaks, neither of them understand what is meant, that is metaphysics.

Voltaire

The point of philosophy is to start with something so simple as not to seem worth stating, and to end with something so paradoxical that no one will believe it.

Bertrand Russell

God offers to every mind its choice between truth and repose. Take which you please—you can never have both.

Ralph Waldo Emerson

Anyone can contemplate the infinite, but somebody has to fix the drains.

To teach how to live with uncertainty, yet without being paralyzed by hesitation, is perhaps the chief thing that philosophy can do.

Bertrand Russell

Is life worth living? This is a question
for an embryo, not for a man.

Samuel Butler

On life's journey faith is nourishment,
virtuous deeds are a shelter, wisdom is
the light by day, and right mindfulness
is the protection by night. If a man lives
a pure life, nothing can destroy him.

Buddha

What is important in life is life,
and not the result of life.

Johann Wolfgang von Goethe

Refrain from asking what is going to happen tomorrow, and every day that fortune grants you, count as gain.

Horace

If you believed more in life, you would fling yourself less to the moment.

Friedrich Nietzsche

Life is nothing but a competition to be the criminal rather than the victim.

Bertrand Russell

The young man who has not wept is a savage, and the old man who will not laugh is a fool.

George Santayana

Life is an end in itself. The only question is whether it is worth living or whether you have grown tired of living it.

The end of life is to be like God, and the soul following God will be like Him.

Socrates

Our chief want in life is somebody who shall make us do what we can.

Ralph Waldo Emerson

Life is one long process of getting tired.

Samuel Butler

Nobody loves life like him that's growing old.

Sophocles

Old age is an incurable disease.

Seneca

Old people like to give good advice,
as solace for no longer being able
to provide bad examples.

François, Duc de La Rochefoucauld

If youth knew; if age could.

Henri Estienne

You must be the change you
wish to see in the world.

Mahatma Gandhi

**The reward of a thing well done is
to have done it.**

Ralph Waldo Emerson

This is my simple religion. There is no need for temples; no need for complicated philosophy. Our own brain, our own heart is our temple; the philosophy is kindness.

Dalai Lama

Either you think or else others have to think for you and take power from you, pervert and discipline your natural tastes, civilize and sterilize you.

F. Scott Fitzgerald

All truly wise thoughts have been
thought already thousands of times;
but to make them truly ours, we must
think them over again honestly, till they
take root in our personal experience.

Johann Wolfgang von Goethe

**Men fear thought as they fear
nothing else on earth, more than
ruin, more even than death.**

Bertrand Russell

Those who cannot remember the past are condemned to repeat it.

George Santayana

I count religion but a childish toy,
And hold there is no sin but ignorance.

Christopher Marlowe

Resolve to be thyself; and know that
who finds himself, loses his misery.

Matthew Arnold

Your work is to discover your world, and then with all your heart give yourself to it.

Buddha

To dare to live alone is the rarest courage; since there are many who had rather meet their bitterest enemy in the field than their own hearts in their closet.

Charles Caleb Colton

I can teach anybody how to get what they want out of life. The problem is that I can't find anybody who can tell me what they want.

Mark Twain

At bottom every man knows well
enough that he is a unique being,
only once on this earth; and by no
extraordinary chance will such a
marvellously picturesque piece of
diversity in unity as he is, ever be
put together a second time.

Friedrich Nietzsche

All the knowledge I possess everyone else can acquire, but my heart is all my own.

Johann Wolfgang von Goethe

I went to the woods because I wished to live deliberately, to front only the essential facts of life, and see if I could not learn what it had to teach, and not, when I came to die, discover that I had not lived.

Henry David Thoreau

Most of our faults are more pardonable than the means we use to conceal them.

François, Duc de La Rochefoucauld

Is life not a hundred times too short for us to stifle ourselves?

Friedrich Nietzsche

Man is least himself when he talks in his own person. Give him a mask, and he will tell you the truth.

Oscar Wilde

It is the chiefest point of happiness that a man is willing to be what he is.

Desiderius Erasmus

To know what you prefer, instead of humbly saying "Amen" to what the world tells you you ought to prefer, is to keep your soul alive.

Robert Louis Stevenson

There is as much difference between us and ourselves as between us and others.

Michel de Montaigne

They must often change, who would be constant in happiness or wisdom.

Confucius

No question is so difficult to answer as that to which the answer is obvious.

George Bernard Shaw

A man's growth is seen in the successive choirs of his friends.

Ralph Waldo Emerson

All men should strive to learn before they die what they are running from, and to, and why.

James Thurber

Living is an illness to which sleep
provides relief every sixteen hours.
It's a palliative. The remedy is death.

Nicolas Chamfort

All truly wise thoughts have been
thought already thousands of times;
but to make them truly ours, we must
think them over again honestly, till they
take root in our personal experience.

Johann Wolfgang von Goethe

Life: a spiritual pickle preserving the
body from decay.

Ambrose Bierce

Order your soul; reduce your wants; live in charity; associate in Christian community; obey the laws; trust in Providence.

Saint Augustine

And thou wilt give thyself relief, if thou doest every act of thy life as if it were the last.

Marcus Aurelius

The contemplative life is often miserable. One must act more, think less, and not watch oneself live.

Nicolas Chamfort

The tragedy of life is not so much what men suffer, but rather what they miss.

Thomas Carlyle

If one considered life as a simple loan, one would perhaps be less exacting. We possess actually nothing; everything goes through us.

Eugène Delacroix

Life has its own hidden forces which you can only discover by living.

Søren Kierkegaard

Life is not an exact science,
it is an art.

Samuel Butler

We must be our own
before we can be another's.

Ralph Waldo Emerson

Every existing thing is born
without reason, prolongs itself out
of weakness, and dies by chance.

Jean-Paul Sartre

May you live
all the days
of your life.
Jonathan Swift

We must welcome the future, remembering
that soon it will be the past; and we must
respect the past, remembering that once it
was all that was humanly possible.

Aldous Huxley

Learn as if you would live forever, live as if
you would die tomorrow.

Mahatma Gandhi

Consider the postage stamp, my son. It
secures success through its ability to stick
to one thing till it gets there.

Josh Billings

Life is the farce which everyone has to perform.

Arthur Rimbaud

As more individuals are produced than can possibly survive, there must…be a struggle for existence, either one individual with another of the same species, or with the individuals of distinct species, or with the physical condition of life.

Charles Darwin

If the doors of perception were cleansed, every thing would appear to man as it is, infinite.

William Blake

Life is like playing a violin solo in public and learning the instrument as one goes on.

Samuel Butler

It is the mark of an educated mind to be able to entertain a thought without accepting it.

Aristotle

Your body is precious. It is our vehicle for awakening. Treat it with care.

Buddha

The man who lets himself be bored is even more contemptible than the bore.

Samuel Butler

Mistakes are the portals of discovery.

James Joyce

I think; therefore I am.

René Descartes

Youth would be an
ideal state if it came
a little later in life.

Herbert Asquith

What a relaxed life is that which
flees the worldly clamor, and
follows the hidden path down
which have gone the few wise men
there have been in the world!

Fray Luis de Leon

There is
no end.
There is no
beginning.
There is only
the infinite
passion of life.
                    Federico Fellini

A Grand
Old Age

To reach old age is part good luck
and part good management.

Do not fear old age: it has its woes,
but also its blessings.

One of the joys of growing older
is having children fight over who
gets to sit on your lap.

Share what life has taught you with others: that they might benefit from your successes as well as your mistakes.

Some elderly people retire, and others, just when they think they've retired, become grandparents.

Old age is a state of mind. So is youth.

If you don't mind being your age, then age doesn't really matter. That is the best example there is of mind over matter.

The youngest souls often inhabit the oldest bodies.

The best
playmate in
the world is a
grandparent.

Our
grandchildren
accept us for
ourselves.

Grandchildren and grandparents
get along because they have
a common enemy.

Each time a child is born, somewhere
there is a grandparent being born, too.

The best fun we can have when we get
older is to become a grandparent.

It is easier for grandparents to become friends with their grandchildren than for parents to do so with their children.

Genes skip generations,
so grandparents find their
grandchildren more likable
than their children.

Grandchildren are perhaps
God's way of compensating
us for the fact we grow old.

Curious how grandparents feel
closer to the generation after
the one they raised.

A grandparent is a baby-sitter who watches the children and not the television.

If nothing is going well, call your grandmother.

Italian proverb

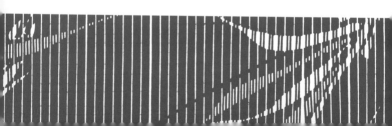

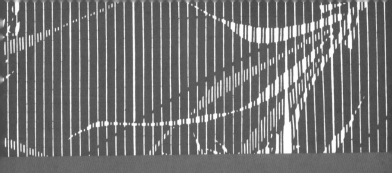

No parent can give a child the same sparkly feeling that a grandparent can.

Grandparents are old on the outside but young on the inside.

To qualify as a grandparent, you need to be able to not recognize your grandchildren when they are disguised.

One moment we are sitting there as a baby on a grown-up's lap, and the next we are the ones with the baby on our lap, and then our baby has a baby in their lap.

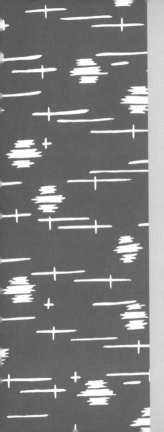

Old age is time we can sit back and enjoy things that we have previously been too busy to appreciate.

The best bridger of the generation gap is a child.

Grandparents need looking after by little children or they get broken.

Maturity is when you are older than a cheese and twice as tasty.

The saddest thing about growing old is losing the urge to throw a snowball at someone.

While you still have the urge, nobody can call you old.

Never stop learning, and never stop laughing.

If you move fast enough, old age won't be able to catch you.

As we get older and a little bit shakier, it is good to remember the lessons of our youth—such as how not to drop the ice cream from your cone!

When your enthusiasm goes, your soul gets wrinkles.

Plenty have grown old and never grown up.

Wrinkles are mementos of
smiles we have had.

Youth is a wonderful thing. What a
crime to waste it on children.

George Bernard Shaw

The years teach much which
the days never knew.

Ralph Waldo Emerson

Numbers are curious things,
especially when it comes to
age. If there were fifteen months
to a year and seventeen years
to a decade, how old would
you feel right now?

Father Time is not always a hard parent, and, though he tarries for none of his children, often lays his hand lightly upon those who have used him well; making them old men and women inexorably enough, but leaving their hearts and spirits young and in full vigor.

Charles Dickens

Middle age has been defined as that time when your age begins to show around your middle.

Life can be pretty unfair. For some, the moment they start to get their head together, their body falls apart.

Life well spent is long.

Leonardo da Vinci

There is a kind of mutual support and respect between children and their grandparents' generation.

The childhood excitement of showing off a new pair of shoes is doubled when showing them to a grandparent.

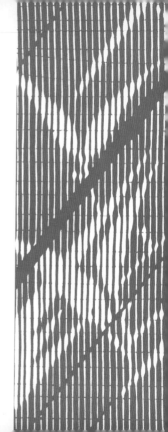

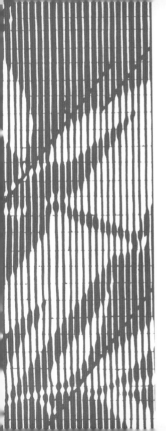

The deck of cards remains the same with age. The shuffling becomes a little slower, that's all.

The price tag for maturity is age, and there's no discount.

The greatest confusion comes from the fact that as we get older our bodies change but we don't.

Hiding your years is rather like asking the leaves on a tree not to change color in fall.

Wear your age proudly; there is nothing sillier that those who try to appear younger than they are.

You can't help getting older, but you don't have to get old.

George Burns

Science has made it possible to live longer, but it hasn't spent anything on developing ways to enjoy being older.

The memory of a life well spent is the greatest aid to a contented old age.

Middle age is when work is a lot less fun and fun is a lot more work.

What most persons consider as virtue, after the age of forty is simply a loss of energy.

Voltaire

It is essential to work on retaining the memory, or our entire life will unhappen before our eyes.

With an active memory we can hold onto all that is and was dear to us.

Remember all that was
good about the past, but
live in the present.

Memories grow
happier with age.

The contents of our memory are the things that we are and all we never want to lose.

With happy memories the garden can be in bloom at any time we like.

Nostalgia is sometimes a vice which is pleasant to indulge in.

We do not remember days; we remember moments from certain days.

When we look back on life, we find that it was simply a series of long and short moments.

The good old days are only ever so in retrospect. These, too, will be the good old days; it's all just a matter of time.

One person's good old days is another person's bad memory.

Nostalgia is like a grammar lesson: you find the present tense and the past perfect.

Nothing rolls back the years like the nose. A gentle waft of scent and we're transported through time and space to an intense memory moment from our childhood.

Laughter is one of the best antidotes to old age; it crosses the generations.

A moment of laughter opens a new world of possibilities.

Even if there is nothing to laugh about, we should laugh on credit.

The days to forget are the ones when nobody laughed.

The only time laughter is unwelcome is when cola is likely to come squirting out of your nose.

Laugh aloud and it will be
like taking a little holiday
from everyday life.

**What soap is to the body,
laughter is to the soul.**

Yiddish proverb

The best sword in a
hopeless battle is laughter.

When
faced
with the
choice of
laughing
or crying,
laugh.

It is easier to deal with anything life throws at us via laughter.

A good bout of laughter rolls back the years.

No man is poor
if he can still laugh.

Laughter is a tranquilizer
with no side effects.

Perhaps I know best why it is man alone who laughs; he alone suffers so deeply that he had to invent laughter.

Friedrich Nietzsche

The great man is he who does not lose his child-heart.

When you become older, don't put away childish things. They'll be required if you want to become a genius.

Every child is an
artist. The problem is
remaining that way.

To the question of your life
you are the answer.
To the problems of your life
you are the solution.

Now, at last, we can begin
to understand ourselves.

Search for your mother's garden,
and you will find your own.

When we are young, the facts are never allowed to get in the way of our imagination. When we get older, our imagination becomes cluttered with unhelpful facts.

If children grew up according to early indications, we should have nothing but geniuses.

Johann Wolfgang von Goethe

Compared to the vibrant, inquisitive, and inventive nature of a child, the average adult appears mentally feeble.

If you want to enjoy life, rediscover the enthusiasm of childhood.

Each day be like a child; make a world that is fresh and new and beautiful. Allow your new day to be full of wonder and excitement.

Scientists should work closely
with children—if they did, we'd
get closer to understanding the
secrets of eternal youth.

A child lives for the here and now,
with little concept of the future and
little need to hold onto the past.

As far as we know we only pass this way once. It's up to us to make sure we get all we can out of the time allotted to us.

Memory and truth are close relatives, rarely twins.

Be patient—live everything
to the full.

**Get up in the morning, go
to bed at night. In between,
occupy yourself as best
you can.**

Make friends and be a
good friend. This is the
height of lasting pleasure.

Be honest in your business and private life. Happiness is dependent upon wisdom, honor, and honesty.

Live a modest life.
Inflated pride, ego,
and boastfulness
have a negative
effect upon our
well-being.

Pursue pleasure wisely. There is
no such thing as a pleasure that
is bad in and of itself.

Treat every day as a gift,
and treasure it for itself.

Meditate—allow your mind peace.

Avoid situations that make you angry. Greed and temptation will all take their toll on the mind and body.

Spend as much time as you can with your family and friends.

Don't dwell on past disappointments, make others feel happy, and you will find happiness yourself.

Enjoy your achievements, but don't rest on your laurels. Always be thinking of new plans. That is the way to keep your mind young.

If you can remember
what it was to be
a child, you are halfway
to staying young.

Learning never ends.
It is a lifelong process.

Don't mistake imagination
for memory.

Above all, enjoy life.

Time has a knack of breaking us in two. Those who survive it take something of the nursery into adulthood with them.

Never be too busy to play—life is too precious to waste in being serious.

If you take an adult and peel back the layers, standing inside is a child waiting to play a game with you.

Rise above the minor irritations of life.

Wrinkles don't hurt.

Accept the fact that you are getting older with grace and dignity.

Try acting your shoe size, not your age.

When grace is joined with wrinkles, it is adorable. There is an unspeakable dawn in happy old age.

Victor Hugo

You've made such an effort to look after yourself and keep your mind and body healthy, once you reach old age you might as well enjoy it.

There is no better age-defying beauty treatment than laughter.

**Rewind the clock,
but don't try to turn
back time.**

Life shouldn't
be valued only
by length—feel
the width.

We become old only
when regrets take
the place of dreams.

Published by MQ Publications Limited
12 The Ivories
6–8 Northampton Street
London
N1 2HY
Tel: 020 7359 2244
Fax: 020 7359 1616
email: mail@mqpublications.com

Text © David Baird 2001
Design Concept: Broadbase
Design: Susannah Good

ISBN: 1 84072 304 1

5 7 9 10 8 6 4

Printed and bound in China